It's OK to be Sad

ISBN: 1-4129-1825-1

Published by Lucky Duck
Paul Chapman Publishing
A SAGE Publications Company
1 Oliver's Yard
55 City Road
London EC1Y 1SP

SAGE Publications, Inc.
2455 Teller Road
Thousand Oaks, California 91320

SAGE Publications India Pvt Ltd.
B-42, Panchsheel Enclave
Post Box 4109
New Delhi 110 017

www.luckyduck.co.uk

Commissioning Editor: Barbara Maines
Editorial Team: Mel Maines, Sarah Lynch, Wendy Ogden
Illustrator: Philippa Drakeford
Designer: Helen Weller

© Margaret Collins 2005

Printed in Great Britain by The Cromwell Press Ltd, Trowbridge, Wiltshire.

It's OK to be Sad

Activities to help children aged 4 to 9 to manage
loss, grief or bereavement

Margaret Collins

Illustrated by Philippa Drakeford

P·C·P
Paul Chapman
Publishing

Lucky Duck is more than a publishing house and training agency. George Robinson and Barbara Maines founded the company in the 1980s when they worked together as a head and as a psychologist, developing innovative strategies to support challenging students.

They have an international reputation for their work on bullying, self-esteem, emotional literacy and many other subjects of interest to the world of education.

George and Barbara have set up a regular news-spot on the website at http://www.luckyduck.co.uk/newsAndEvents/viewNewsItems

and information about their training programmes can be found at www.insetdays.com

More details about Lucky Duck can be found at http://www.luckyduck.co.uk

Visit the website for all our latest publications in our specialist topics:

- Emotional Literacy
- Self-esteem
- Bullying
- Positive Behaviour Management
- Circle Time
- Anger Management
- Asperger's Syndrome
- Eating Disorders.

Contents

A note on the use of gender

Rather than repeat throughout the book the modern but cumbersome 's/he', we have decided to use both genders equally throughout the range of activities. In no way are we suggesting a stereotype for either gender in any activity. We believe that you can adapt if the example you are given does not correspond to the gender of the child in front of you!

A note on the use of the words 'family' and 'parents'

Many children do not live in conventional two parent families. Some are looked after by the local authority and might have confusing and painful experiences. We often use the term 'carer' to identify the adults who look after such a child or young person. Sometimes 'people you live with' might be more appropriate than 'family'. These phrases can make the text rather repetitive. Please use the words most suitable for the young people you work with.

Introduction

Children are going to face loss, grief and bereavement at some time in their lives. They will need help in learning to understand how to deal with the feelings that loss, whether trivial or serious, generates. It is not sufficient only to attend to a child's needs when an event has caused pain. Preparation for, and understanding of, the needs of people suffering from loss and grief can be part of your personal, social, health and citizenship education (PSHCE) programme. With very young children this can be most effectively achieved in whole-class sessions, perhaps in Circle Time, using stories, discussion and activities.

> 'Evidence has shown that it is possible to identify the factors that have an impact on children's mental health. Certain individuals and groups are more at risk of developing mental health problems than others, and these risks are located in a number of areas – risks specific to the children, to their family, their environment and life events. There are a range of factors in children's and young people's lives which can result in them being at increased risk of developing mental health difficulties: loss or separation resulting from death, parental separation, divorce, hospitalisation, loss of friendships especially in adolescence, family breakdowns that results in the child having to live elsewhere.'

> Promoting Children's Mental Health within Early Years and School Settings. DfEE June 2001 1.2 page 8

> *In childhood the range of depressive symptoms may include refusal or reluctance to attend school, irritability, abdominal pain and headache. p35*

> *Children who are depressed often present with non-specific symptoms such as physical complaints, irritability, withdrawal, or they may express feeling unhappy or miserable. p34*

> *Factors which make children and young people vulnerable to depression include: family breakdown, death or loss of a loved one, neglect, abuse, bullying and other adverse life events. p35*

This book does not offer counselling or specific activities for children who are bereaved. It is a programme of activities for use in PSHCE to use with the whole class. It is a preparation for loss and bereavement and a way of helping children to understand the feelings of people who grieve rather than a tool to use when a child is bereaved.

Many families nowadays do not consist of two parents and some children. Some parents work and live away for some of the time; some separate or divorce and share the upbringing of their children; some parents form new relationships that generate new step or half families. All these situations can create feelings of loss, anger and grief within the children. Many of these children feel it is their fault; some work very hard at trying to bring parents together again.

Other children are bereaved and face an irreversible and lifelong loss when one or more of their parents die. While arrangements will have been made for the wellbeing of the child, her life will have been turned upside down by the trauma and the complete change of lifestyle. She will need a teacher sensitive to her feelings, who can help other children to relate to this child in a way that will help her to accept the loss and move on. They will all need to understand that it is OK for the child to feel sad when overwhelmed by grief. A programme of activities such as detailed here will help all the class to be prepared; ready to understand another child's feelings in her loss.

The first activities gently lead the children into the theme of loss, grief and separation with only the final activities concerned with death. They will give the children permission to cry – to help them to know that it is OK to feel sad, angry and hurt, while understanding that often there is nothing that can be done to change the situation.

You may choose to do the activities in any order according to the needs of the children in your class, omitting any that you feel are too sensitive for your particular children to handle at any one time.

Picture storybooks

Using stories is a wonderful way of conveying emotion and feelings without putting the children themselves in the frame. They can empathise with the characters without becoming too involved. For this reason all the activities in this book start with either a scenario or a story from a published picture storybook. Nearly all of these books will already be in the school or classroom library. If not, the central library will certainly have a copy for you to borrow. At the end of this book you'll find full details of these books in a list together with details of other appropriate picture storybooks, each with a précis of the story, for you to use with children in story time or Circle Time.

When you are using a picture storybook, try to immerse everyone in the story by reading it through once without pausing. Then break down the story into scenarios and talk about what everyone did and how the characters were feeling in the different stages of the story. Encourage the children to suggest alternative actions that might have changed the outcome of the story by using 'What if…' questions, especially questions such as, 'What if you'd been there, what would you have done or said?' Having finally unravelled the story and discovered what the characters felt, as a final activity go back to the beginning and enjoy it through once more.

Should you have a child in class who has been bereaved you can use some of the activities to help other children to empathise with him, always being careful and sensitive to the bereaved child's needs. Young children seem to have no difficulty in using the words 'dead', 'died' and 'death'. It is we adults who seek to wrap up the event in more carefully acceptable euphemisms. You may choose to expand the children's learning by talking about the funeral and burial arrangements in various religions. These are not mentioned in this book, but you may wish to include them in your teaching of various religions, especially if such a sad occasion arises.

Use the activities as your main theme in your Circle Time sessions. You could use one activity each week, or pick out those more appropriate to the needs of your children. For example, if someone comes to school feeling very sad that her pet has died you could sensitively read the story *I'll Always Love You*; go through the activities in 'I'll love you every day' and do the activity sheet. When someone has a new family you could read the picture storybook *Grace and Family* and use the activities and activity sheet about 'Claire's Family'. You can also use the story of *Snow White* to challenge the stereotyping of step-mothers, step-fathers and step-sisters.

Circle Time

Teachers who already use Circle Time with their young children will have Circle Time rules in place as well as strategies for making this an active time. Teachers who do not use Circle Time and want to incorporate this into their teaching will need to set up rules for Circle Time as well as establishing a welcoming opening activity and fun game or singing closing activity.

Throughout this book the activities include various actions that will help to break up the monotony of sitting in a circle for too long. It is important to put movement into Circle Time and some activities ask children to move out of the circle to work in pairs or in their working groups to draw, write, role-play or talk about the topic. The following are more detailed explanations of moving strategies used in the activities in this book.

Question and answer: The teacher starts by asking a question and the first child answers it before in turn asking the next child the same question.

Finish the sentence: You give the children a starter by saying the sentence yourself and finding a bland response, for example, for the sentence, 'I think he would feel…' you might supply the easy word 'sad'. The next child in the circle now says the sentence supplying their own ending. Every child is expected to supply some ending, but you can allow children to 'pass', If you do this, give them another chance to supply an ending when everyone has had a turn.

Pass the face: The first child shows by his face how he feels, turns to show the next child who turns to show the next person, and so on around the circle.

Stand and show: Children sit in the circle with their pictures; the first stands up to show his work, then sits down before the next child stands.

Change places: Children are asked to finish sentences, or offer phrases. When someone else offers the same response, the second child is asked to change places with the one who first said it. If several children give the same response later children can change places with the one who said it last.

Jot down: It is useful to have a notebook to jot down any of the appropriate words or phrases the children offer. You can read through these words later in the activity or make word banks by listing and displaying the words under an appropriate heading.

Hands up: Children are invited to raise a hand to offer their contribution.

Pass: Make sure that children know they can say 'pass' if they have no contribution to make. Give them a chance at the end to offer anything they have thought of.

Vote with your feet: Ask children to go and stand in various parts of the room to show which of the choices they wish to vote for. (For example, those who choose the option A, go and stand by the window, those who choose B stand by the board, those who choose C stand by the door.)

Count yourselves: Ask the children to stand in a line and, starting at one end of the line, to count themselves with the first child saying 'one', the second saying 'two' and so on.

Classroom displays

Some activities ask children to draw pictures which you can choose to display; some ask children to make a class picture. Make these displays interactive by adding questions or information in speech bubbles. Read the writing (reading practice) and refer to the display as occasions occur in the classroom. Share these displays with other children in the school or with the children's families. You could also share them with the whole school as part of a class assembly.

Activity sheets and CD-ROM

Each lesson has an accompanying activity sheet of the same name which can be accessed via the CD-ROM. If you wish to photocopy them directly from the book you need to set your photocopier to 125% in order to make A4 copies.

Some activity sheets rely on the lesson activity, which must be done first; others are a more personal extension to the theme of the lesson activity. The activity sheets have been kept as simple as possible with the same format repeated in each one. Several have a wordbox with suggestions of words the child may need in order to complete the activity sheet. It is not intended that each child uses these words, but they might help children with ideas and spellings of words they might need. Space has been left for you, the teacher, to add spellings of words the child might ask for. At the end, there is a 'turn over' drawing and writing activity for the children to do on the other side of the paper. This open activity can act as differentiation so that able children can engage in more challenging work.

You can use the sheet in various ways. Use it as:

▸ a new idea to put the child himself in the activity

▸ a theme for further work

▸ an extension to the lesson

▸ a piece of work for the children to take home to show their families.

I Lost My Toy

Start with the picture book *Dogger*, by Shirley Hughes.

In Circle Time read the story to the children all the way through. It is about Dave who loves this soft toy Dogger to the exclusion of all his other toys. At bedtime after a busy day out Dogger is nowhere to be found and despite several searches

Dave felt...

really happy
he wanted to cuddle Dogger
he wanted to go to bed
comfortable
happy
really glad.

Dave has to go to bed without him. The following day at a school summer fair, Dogger is found on one of the stalls, but before Dave can buy him someone else does. However all ends happily through the unselfishness of Dave's sister Bella.

After finishing the story ask the children to think about how Dave felt about his toy every night at bedtime. Ask them to finish the sentence:

'I think Dave felt…' and collect their responses to talk about later. Ask children who repeat what someone else has said to change places with that child.

Now ask the children how they think Dave felt at bedtime the day that Dogger was missing. Ask volunteers to give you words that you can use to make another list.

Read through the two lists and talk about the opposite feelings in them lists. Ask the children to think about how Dave looked when he lost Dogger. Ask the children to 'pass the face' around the circle.

Talk with the children about whether Dave would give up hope of finding Dogger. How many think that Dave thought Dogger was lost for ever? Ask volunteers to say what they think Dave's mum would have said and done to cheer him up. What might Bella, his sister, have been able to do?

Ask the children to find paper and crayons and to draw a picture of Dave trying to find Dogger. Can they draw some of the places where he would have looked? Ask them to turn over their paper and to draw Dave at the school fair when he saw Dogger on the stall. Ask the children to bring their pictures into the circle and to 'stand and show' both their pictures to the whole class.

Dave is looking everywhere for Dogger.

Now ask the children to think about themselves in this story and what they could have done to help. What could they have done and said to try to cheer Dave up? Ask them to finish the sentence: 'I could have…'

Ask them to think about how Dave felt when he didn't have enough money to buy Dogger from the stall. Ask volunteers to tell the class and make a list of these feelings. How do they think Dave felt when someone else bought Dogger? Ask volunteers to tell the group and make a list of these feelings. Are any of them the same feelings? Display these two lists so that the children can use the words in their writing. Go around the circle, asking the children, in turn, to use one of these words in a sentence.

Remind the children how Bella got Dogger back for Dave. Ask them to think about what he could have said to her.

Thank you, Bella.

You are so kind to me.

You are a super sister.

Read through the story again, stopping at all the places where Dave's feelings have been explored through these activities.

Ask the children to draw another picture of Dave feeling great and happy about having Dogger back again and then do activity sheet 'I Lost My Toy'.

Remind the children that it's OK to feel sad and even to want to cry when you lose something precious.

I Lost My Toy

Draw one of your best toys:

These will help

My best toy is ....

How would you feel if you lost this toy?

I would feel

....

....

Turn over.

What would you do? Draw and write what you would do.

A Sleepover

Read this story in Circle Time.

Brendan was five years old and loved going to visit his Grandma. She lived just two stops away along the railway line and before he started going to school Brendan used to go there often. Now he was at school he didn't see Grandma very often, so you can imagine how he felt when his mum said that he was going to stay with Grandma overnight. She explained that she and Dad were going to have a special evening out and that they wouldn't be back home until very late. They would both come to collect Brendan the next morning.

Brendan put his pyjamas in his little case alongside his teddy. Mum put in a spare set of clothes and his toothbrush and Brendan could hardly wait to get to Grandma's house. Mum came in to have a cup of tea and then kissed Brendan and Grandma goodbye and they went to the door to wave her off.

Brendan and Grandma went back inside and did a jigsaw and then they had tea. It did feel strange to have Grandma bathing him and putting him to bed. She read him a story, said goodnight and left the door open and the landing light on. Then Brendan began to think about home; he began to miss Mum and Dad…

Talk to the children about how Brendan would feel as he lay in bed thinking about home and missing his mum and dad. Ask them to finish the sentence:

'I think Brendan might be feeling…

Allow children to pass.

Jot down the words the children give you and tick any repeats. When everyone has had a turn, read out your lists of feelings words and ask if anyone can think of more feelings to add.

'I think Brendan might be feeling...'

10 said sad
8 said unhappy
4 said he would cry
1 said missing home
2 said afraid
1 said uncomfortable
1 said worried
1 said will she come back

Ask the children to think about what Grandma could do to make Brendan feel better about missing his mum. Ask anyone who has an idea to stand up. Ask each of these children, in turn, to tell the class what they think.

Ask the children to get a piece of paper and to draw a picture of Brendan's Grandma helping him to feel better. Help them to write a caption for their picture. Ask them to bring their picture back to the circle to show the rest of the class and to read their caption. Ask them to 'stand and show'.

Talk about what the children have drawn and written.

Now ask the children to think about how Brendan might feel in the morning when his mum and dad came back to see him. Jot down these words and later write a list of them under the heading 'Happy feelings' to display on the wallboard.

Do the children think that he would tell them that:

▸ he had been unhappy and missing them

▸ he had cried

▸ that Grandma had to comfort him

▸ he was worried that they might not come for him?

Ask the children to draw another picture, this time of Mum and Dad coming to collect Brendan. Ask them to suggest a caption or a title for their picture, or to write some of the happy words around it.

You could read *Don't Forget to Write* by Martina Selway and use activity sheet 'A sleepover'.

12

My name is ....

A Sleepover

Would you like to sleepover at a friend's house? Yes ☐ No ☐
Draw yourself sleeping at a friend's house.

This is me sleeping at .... house

How do you feel?

I feel

....

....

Would you miss your family? Yes ☐ No ☐

Turn over.
Draw a picture of yourself with your family.
Write about your picture.

A Lost Pet

Read this scenario in Circle Time.

Jill lived with her mum and dad, one brother Joe who was 12 years old and a sister Alice who was nine. They had a lovely black and white collie dog. When the dog had been very small, he was always playing in the garden, getting all dusty, so that's what they called him. All the children loved Dusty and played with him and told him their secrets. He came into the house during the day when everyone made a fuss of him. At night Dusty slept in a kennel in a big fenced run in the garden. Sometimes he stayed there when the family had to go somewhere where they couldn't take him. Every day after school Jill, Alice and Joe put Dusty on a lead and took him for a walk. Then they fed him and made sure he had clean water; it was Joe's responsibility to make sure he was shut up securely at night in his run.

One morning when Joe went to let Dusty out he found a hole in the fencing. Dusty was not there.

Talk to the children about how the children and their family would feel when they found that Dusty had gone. Ask them to finish the sentence:

'I think they would feel…'

Jot down these words to use later.

Ask volunteers to say what the family could do to try to get Dusty back again and write these up on the flip-chart.

I think they could…

telephone the police
go and ask neighbours
put a notice in the shop window
put a notice on lamp-posts
tell everyone at school
offer a reward
put some food out in case he came back
tell the people who look after dogs in dog's homes.

Ask the children to think which would be the very best thing and to vote on it. Use the strategy 'Vote with your feet'. Ask them to count themselves.

Ask the children to think of a good ending to the story. Ask volunteers to tell the class. Jot down what they say and talk about each one – would they work? Are they sensible things to do? Could anyone get hurt?

Ask the children to work in pairs to draw a picture or write their good ending.

Ask the children to come back into the circle and to 'stand and show' their pictures to the whole class.

A good ending

Dusty came home all by himself. He was very glad to be back because he was hungry. The children were so happy.

Ask the children to think of words to tell you how they would feel if Dusty was their dog and came back after being lost. Ask them to work in pairs and to write down as many feelings words as they can. Ask the pairs to join up with their group and put all their words together on one list. Come together in the circle and ask a spokesperson from each group to read out their list.

Make one list of all the words. Look at the first list they made – how they would feel when Dusty was gone. Can the children find opposites? Are any words almost the same? Ask someone to make two lists using the computer and display these 'feelings' words for the children to use when they are doing other writing.

Talk to the children about these feelings words. Explain that when something is lost, people will feel sad and unhappy. Some people might cry; others might think it was their fault and feel angry. Talk about how everyone would have felt if Dusty had not been found. Explain that sometimes there is no happy ending; if so we are allowed to cry and to be sad about it. You could use activity sheet 'A Lost Pet' now.

A Lost Pet

Have you got a pet? Yes ☐ No ☐

Draw a pet you would like to have.

I would like to have a ....

How would you keep your pet safe and happy?

I would

....

....

Turn over.
How would you feel if your pet got lost? What would you do?
Draw how you would feel and what you would do.

Where's My Purse?

In Circle Time tell the children the story of Julia, who lost her purse.

> Julia was seven years old and she had been saving up to buy her mum a birthday present. She knew just what she was going to buy, a blue vase she had seen in the supermarket when they had been shopping. She asked her big sister to take Mum off to look at something else while she bought it, but when she put her hand in her pocket for her purse, it had gone. She and her sister went to the Customer Services desk and told the lady there, but no-one had found it. Julia might have lost it on the way.

Ask the children if they have ever lost something precious like this. Ask volunteers to finish the sentence: 'I once lost… and I felt…' Jot down what these children say they have lost. At the end read out the list to remind the children and then ask them all to think how Julia felt and to 'pass the face' around the circle.

Ask the children to kneel up if they think Julia cried when she found she had lost it. Ask them to count themselves. Ask them to stand up if they think they would have cried if they had been Julia. Ask them to count themselves again. Which is the greater number? Ask volunteers to say why they think this is.

Ask the children to think about whether crying is a good idea. Will that make her feel better? Explain that crying can help to make you feel better, though it won't bring the purse back. Ask the children to think what Julia can do now about her mother's birthday. Ask them to finish the sentence: 'Julia could…'

Julia could:

look everywhere for it
ask her sister to lend her some money
make Mum a present
make Mum a card
tell Mum
give Mum a promise present
give Mum a helping hand.

Ask the children to think of something precious to them – a book, a toy or game. Ask them if losing this special thing would make them feel sad and want to cry. Ask them to put a hand up if it would make them want to cry.

Ask them to close their eyes; think of this special thing and to think how they would feel if they lost it. Ask them to open their eyes and finish this sentence: 'If I lost my… I would feel…'

I would feel...

sad

upset

angry

fed up

worried

cross

annoyed with myself

careless.

Explain that it's OK to feel sad, or to cry, especially if it makes you feel better and it brings other people to come to help. However crying won't help to bring back the thing they have lost. Ask them to think of what they could do if they lost this special thing. Ask them to get paper and crayons and draw a picture of what they would do.

Back in the circle ask the children to 'stand and show' their pictures. Talk about what the children's pictures show they would do. Are all these things sensible things to do? Could any be dangerous? Could any be a bad thing to do? Ask the children to help you to make a list of the good, sensible things to do if they have lost anything precious.

Remind the children that there are ways of helping themselves to feel better when things go wrong like this. Ask volunteers to say what they do to make themselves feel better. Make a list of these things. Have they included;

- ▶ talking to someone about it

- ▶ trying to be more careful next time?

Ask the children to think up a good ending to the story of Julia and the purse. Ask them to work in pairs to decide a good ending and to draw and write about it. You could use activity sheet, 'Where's My Purse?' now.

Where's My Purse?

Wordbox

asked

looked

thought

worries

everywhere

help

Draw a picture of Julia in the supermarket when she lost her purse.

What did Julia do?

I think Julia

....

....

....

Turn over.

Draw a picture of yourself with your special toy or game.
Write what you would do if you lost it.

Missing You

Tell the children this story about Azif and Brett.

All the children in Class 3 like Azif. He is a happy boy who is friendly to everyone. He has a best friend called Brett and they are inseparable. They live near to each other in the same street and play together after school and at the weekends. One Monday morning Azif comes to school with a gloomy face. In the playground, everyone crowds around him to ask what the matter is. He says he has a letter for the teacher to tell her that he is moving to a new place to live and will go to a new school. Brett says he doesn't believe it; he says his parents would have told him. He says that Azif's parents would never want to go to live somewhere else.

They go into the classroom and Azif gives the letter to the teacher. Mrs Ashworth is very sad as she tells the children that Azif will be leaving their school at the end of the week.

Talk to the children about this situation and ask them to think about how Brett is feeling. Can they think of words to describe his feelings? Ask them to finish the sentence:

'Brett would be feeling…'

Jot down these words.

Ask volunteers to give words to describe how Azif would be feeling and make a list of these. Are they the same words?

Talk to the children about how people feel when their friends go away. If someone has left your class, talk about this person and how she felt. Explain that there are always good reasons why people move away and have a 'hands up' session to find examples. Talk about these good reasons.

Brett would be feeling...

angry
let down
upset
he won't believe it
he won't let it happen
he wants to go with Azif
lonely
no-one to be special friends with.

Ask the children to think about what Brett did and said when he got home. What would he actually say to his parents? Ask the children to work in pairs and role-play this situation with one child being Brett and the other someone in his family. Come back into the circle and ask volunteers to show their role-play to the class. Did any of the children suggest ways in which the two boys could keep their friendship going?

Ask the children to think of ways to stay friends with someone when one of them has to go away to a new home and a new school. Collect their ideas to make a list.

You could...

write letters
make cards
send emails
send photos
phone them
have visits
make a video to send
go on holiday together
spend half-term holidays at each others' homes.

Make a class picture

Ask the children to draw themselves as large as they can on a piece of A4 paper. Ask them to cut out their pictures of themselves. Choose one of the pictures to be Brett and one to be Azif. Ask children to help you to make a background to put all these children and Brett on one side and Azif by himself on the other side. Help the children to make speech bubbles to put on the picture between the children and Azif, to show what Brett, Azif and the other children are saying about keeping in touch.

Explain to the children that it's OK to be sad if a friend is going away. They can't change this, but they can use lots of ways to keep in touch.

You might like the children to do the activity sheet 'Missing You' now.

class picture

I'll call you

I'll write

I'll send photos

You can visit

Missing You

Draw one of your friends here. Write your friend's name: ....

How would you feel if this friend had to go away to another house and school? I would feel

....

....

What would you say to this friend?
I would say

....

....

Turn over.
Draw yourself saying goodbye to this friend. Write in a speech bubble what you both would say.

Moving House

Tell the children the story of Jessica, who is leaving her home and friends behind.

> When Jessica's parents tell her that they are moving to a new house Jessica feels angry and sad. Jessica shouts that she doesn't want to go anywhere else and says she will ask if she can stay behind and live at her best friend Alice's house. Jessica's parents explain that Dad has a new job and they must move to be near to his workplace. They say that they will all go and look at some houses at the weekend and that Jessica can see which house she likes best. They say they know the school that they want Jessica to go to and she will be able to see it from the outside. Jessica doesn't want to go. She just sits and sobs and says that she isn't going; she likes this house where she has lived ever since she was born, she likes her school – she has all her friends there, especially her best friend Alice who she's known since she was a baby.

Ask the children to give you words that describe how they think that Jessica really feels about leaving her house and school. Ask them to finish the sentence: 'I think Jessica feels…' Jot down the words the children say and use 'change places' for repeats.

Ask the children to think of all the things they could say to Jessica to help her to feel better about having to move to a new house and school.

Ask them to work in pairs and write down what they could say to help Jessica to feel better about having to move.

Ask each pair to read out their suggestions to their group and talk about them before choosing a volunteer from the group to read them all out to the rest of the class. Will any of them work well? Will some not work?

Jessica feels…

sad
upset
angry
cross
annoyed
fed up
worried
anxious
won't like it
will miss everyone
will hate it there.

Ask the children to raise a hand if they have ever had to leave a house and move to a new one. Count how many.

Ask these children to tell the others how they felt. Jot down what they say and then ask other children to think of how they would feel if they had to leave their house and all their friends behind to move to a new house and school.

Ask them to make a face to show how they would feel and to 'pass the face' around the circle.

Ask them to finish the sentence: 'I would feel…' Jot down their responses to make a list. Did anyone say they would feel excited and look forward to moving?

When everyone has had a turn, read out the list. Ask the children to choose the three best sentences; write them up somewhere for the children to see and copy.

Ask them to choose the one sentence that best says how they would feel, to write the sentence on their paper and draw a picture of themselves feeling just like that. Explain that it is OK to feel sad or angry when you have to do something that you don't want to do, but tell them feeling like this won't change things.

Ask the children to work in their groups and write down all the good things they can think of about moving house. Share these with the class. Do they all agree?

You could use the activity sheet, 'Moving House' now.

Moving House

Have you ever moved house? Yes ☐ No ☐
Draw a picture of the three people or things you
would miss most if you had to move house.

friend

garden

park

**playing
field**

**swimming
pool**

cubs

I would miss ....

I would miss ....

I would miss ....

Why would you miss these people or things?
I would miss them because

....

....

Turn over.
Draw yourself telling Jessica all the good things about moving
house. Write all these good things down.

I Won't Forget You

Start with the picture book *Leaving Mrs. Ellis* by Catherine Robinson.

In Circle Time read the story all the way through. It is about Leo who realises that he is moving to a new class soon and will have to say goodbye to Mrs Ellis. Leo's Mum makes a chocolate cake for her, to say thank you for being his teacher. His new teacher will be Mrs Lyons; he thinks she will be a scary person and has bad dreams. Then he meets Mrs Lyons in the supermarket, paints her a picture and realises that he has nothing to be afraid of.

Ask the children to tell you which part of the story they liked best. Go around the circle with 'question and answer': 'I liked the bit where... Which part did you like?' Encourage children not to pass.

I felt unhappy when I had a new doctor. I liked the old one.

Unhappy

When everyone has had a turn ask them think about how Leo felt when he realised that he would be leaving Mrs Ellis' class. Ask volunteers to give words to describe how Leo felt. Jot these down to make a list.

Read through your list and, as you read each word, ask the children to put up a hand if they have ever felt like this. Ask some of the volunteers to say what made them feel like that.

Out of the circle ask the children to choose one word from the list and to draw themselves when they once felt like that. Ask them to write the word under their picture and write where they were, and who they were with when they felt like that.

Ask the children to remember how they felt before they came into your class. Did they leave a teacher at your school behind? Did they leave someone behind at nursery? Did they leave Mum behind when they came into your class? Ask the children to think about how they felt then and to think about how they feel now.

Ask them to get a piece of A4 paper and fold it in half. Show them how to label one half 'Then' and the other half 'Now'. Ask them to draw themselves how they were feeling when they left their old class or at home in the 'Then' half of the paper and to draw themselves as they feel now in the other half.

Ask the children to come to the circle and to 'stand and show' their pictures.

Remind the children that it is OK to feel sad when they leave someone behind and miss them, but remind them that they can remember them with love.

You could use activity sheet, 'I Won't Forget You' now.

My name is ....

I Won't Forget You

Draw someone who comes to visit you.

Wordbox

kind

present

take

out

miss

love

remember

What do you like about this person?
I like

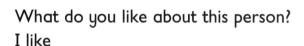

....

....

How do you feel when they go?
I feel

....

....

Turn over.
Draw yourself waving them goodbye when they go. Write what you will say to them.

I Don't Know Anyone Here

Tell the children this story about Jacob who is moving into a new school.

Jacob hated leaving his old house and school in England. He had lived there ever since he was born and had loads of friends and knew everyone. When his family decided to move to Scotland he was angry at first but he knew he would have to get used to it. His dad's job had moved and they had to move with it.

Now he is starting a new school and he hates it because everyone knows everyone else and he feels the odd one out. He doesn't know the shopkeepers and he doesn't know the town. He is afraid he might get lost and holds on to his mum's hand very tightly when they go out.

Jacob's mum is very kind and she knows how he is feeling, so she sits down and talks to Jacob about how he can make new friends and stop feeling so bad about leaving his old friends behind. But Jacob doesn't want to be friends with new children. He just misses his old friends and he keeps feeling really sad. What can his mum do to help him?

Ask the children what they think Jacob's mum can do to help him. In a 'hands up' session, ask them to say what they think she can do. Jot down what the children say and at the end talk about their suggestions.

Ask the children to think about what Jacob can do to help himself to make new friends. Ask them to finish the sentence: 'I think Jacob can…' Jot down what the children say. Talk about both these lists about what his mother and Jacob can both do. Are some ideas on both lists? Which will work best?

His mum can…

take him swimming to meet people
let him join Cub Scouts
ask people to come to tea
ask his teacher to help
go to the local church
join an after school club
help with football so he could join in.

Ask volunteers to tell how they think Jacob might be feeling when he thinks about his old friends. How does he feel about them when he is trying to make new friends at his new home and school? Ask the children to think about what Jacob can do to keep in touch with his old friends.

Talk to the children about other people who can help Jacob. What could his old teacher do? What could his new teacher do? Ask the children to think about these two teachers. Ask them to get a piece of paper and fold it down the middle. On one half ask them to write 'Jacob's old teacher' and on the other write 'Jacob's new teacher'. Ask them to draw and write what these two teachers could do to help Jacob.

Jacob's old teacher	Jacob's new teacher
She could keep in touch by sending letters and photos.	He could find a buddy to help Jacob to settle in.

Remind them that the children in Jacob's new school have a part to play to befriend Jacob and include him in their games. Ask the children what they could do to help Jacob if he were in their class. Ask them to work in pairs and to role-play the situation with one being Jacob and the other a buddy. In Circle Time talk about the role-plays. Are there any good ideas?

You could use the activity sheet, 'I Don't Know Anyone Here' now.

I Don't Know Anyone Here

Draw Jacob and his buddy here.

Wordbox

show

coats

library
books

play

share

befriend

help

kind

I'm your buddy

What is the buddy doing to help Jacob?
The buddy is

....

....

....

Turn over.
Draw Jacob feeling better. Write down what helped him to feel better.

Letting Go

In Circle Time, tell the children the story of Sara's sister Amy who is leaving home to go to college.

Sara lived with her mum and her big sister Amy in a small flat in the centre of town. They had lived there as long as Sara could remember; all three of them. Sara's sister Amy was quite a lot older than Sara and would be leaving school soon. She had always been there for Sara, helping her with her work, taking her out and helping to choose her clothes while their mother was at work.

One day Amy comes home to tell them that she has decided what she wants to do in the future. She wants to go to college to learn how to be a teacher. Sara can't understand it at first. 'You mean you'll go away and sleep away and never come back?' she says. 'Of course I'll come back.' says Amy, 'but not every night and not every week. I'll not be going until after the holidays and even then I'll be home for Christmas.' That night as Sara lies in bed trying to sleep she feels as though her life is changing. No Amy to help her and be with her, just herself and Mum. 'It won't be the same at all,' she thinks.

Ask the children to think about this situation. Amy will be going away to live in a different place and find new friends. Her new world will be exciting and adventurous. Sara will be left behind. How is Amy going to manage this big change in her life? Ask volunteers to tell you how they think Sara will feel.

Ask them to think about what Sara can do to keep in touch with Amy.
Ask them to finish the sentence: 'I think Sara could…' Jot down what the children say to make a list and then read it through to them. Ask them to think which one is the best thing to do. Ask them to 'vote by their feet' and to count themselves.

> We voted on the best thing for Sara to do…
>
> 12 say write to her
> 8 say text her
> 5 say email her
> 4 say phone her
> 1 said fax her
> 1 said use a webcam.

Now talk about the sadness that Sara will feel as she misses her big sister.

Ask volunteers to tell you what kinds of things Sara can do to help her to get over missing her sister.

Make a list of these things and talk about the ones that would be best to do.

Ask the children to think what Sara's mum would be feeling when Amy decided to go to college. Would she be happy for her? Would she be proud of her? Would she miss her?

Explain to the children that life changes suddenly sometimes and that when it does we have to try to manage the change by thinking of the other people and by deciding the best thing we can do. Explain that Sara has to let her sister go without making her feel unhappy at leaving Sara and her mum behind.

Sara could...

join a club
learn a sport
learn a skill – knit, sew, cook
invite a friend home
talk about it to her friend
think about Amy being happy
help her mother more
talk to her mother more
be more responsible
look after herself more
look forward to Amy's visit
make cards for Amy
show Amy she is growing up.

Ask the children to draw a picture of Sara and her Mum saying good-bye to Amy as she leaves to go to college. Will they have sad faces or happy faces?

Remind the children that it's OK to feel sad as long as they realise they can't change what is going to happen. Sometimes we have to let people go and then they will come back and visit. Ask the children to do the activity sheet 'Letting Go' now.

Letting Go

Draw a picture of Sara and her mum helping
Amy to get her things ready to go to college.

What would you say to Sara about letting her sister go?
I would say

....

....

....

Turn over.
Draw a picture of Amy coming home for a visit at Christmas.
Write in speech bubbles how Mum and Amy and Sara will feel.

I'll Love You Every Day

Start with the picture book *I'll Always Love You*, by Hans Wilhelm.

This is the story of a boy and his dog Effie. Effie is a puppy but grows faster than the boy. They have a lovely life together but while the boy grows slowly Effie quickly grows older and one day becomes ill. Even the vet can't help to make Effie better. Every night the boy remembers to say to Effie, 'I'll always love you.' Effie dies and everyone is sad. His family never told Effie that they loved her but it helps the boy when he remembers that he told her every night that he loved her.

Ask the children to think about the boy and his family. Ask them to decide who loved Effie the most – was it the mum or dad, the brother or sister or the boy? Ask the children to 'vote with their feet' and to count themselves.

Ask the children to think about the dog Effie. Do they think that Effie knew that the boy loved her? Ask the children to put a thumb up for 'yes' and a thumb down for 'no'.

Can the children suggest how the boy showed that he loved Effie. Ask volunteers to tell you and make a list of what they say.

Ask the children to think about the other people in the family, those who didn't tell Effie that they loved her. Explain that Effie would know that they loved her, even if they didn't say so, because they would have shown their love, but how might they feel when she had died and it was too late to tell her?

He would...

play with her
give her water
feed her
clean her dish
take her for walks
cuddle her
talk to her
brush her coat
buy her a collar.

Ask the children to kneel up if they have a pet. Ask these pet owners to say 'yes' or 'no' when you ask them if they tell their pet that they love them. Ask these pet owners to tell you how they show their pet that they love them.

Ask the children to close their eyes and think about the last time they told someone that they loved them. Ask them to make a picture inside their heads of this person and themselves and what they are doing when they say that they love them. Ask them to open their eyes and to finish the sentence: 'On... day I told... that I loved them.' Encourage children not to pass.

Ask the children to draw a picture of this person and to write why they love them.

Explain that telling people that we love them isn't quite enough; we need to show people that we love them too.

Ask them to think of ways they can show this person that they love them. Ask them to finish the sentence: 'I show... that I love them when I...'

I love my brother because he helps me.

Ask the children to bring their pictures to the circle and to 'stand and show' them. Remind them that it is important to tell people that we love them and remind them that in the story the boy told Effie every day.

You could use the activity sheet, 'I'll Love You Every Day' now.

I'll Love You Every Day

Draw yourself with a person or a pet that you love.

How do you show that you love this person or pet?
I show them I love them when I

....

....

....

Turn over.
Draw yourself loving this person or pet.
Write how you would feel if they went away.

We Are Missing You

In Circle Time talk to the children about people who have to go to hospital because they are very ill. Explain that sometimes patients stay in hospital just a short time, a day or so, but that sometimes people are very ill and have to stay in hospital for a very long time. Help them to understand the word 'patient'.

Ask them to close their eyes and think about someone in their family having to go away to hospital because they are very ill. Ask volunteers to say how they think this patient would feel about having to go away to hospital and leave their family at home.

They would feel...

ill
they want to get well
sad
upset
worried
missing their family
no friends
lonely
strange
not know what to do
they want to go home.

What could they do to show they loved this patient who was ill? Ask them to finish the sentence: 'I could...'

Ask the children to think about the things a visitor could do and what a visitor could say. Ask the children to work in pairs and role-play a hospital situation. Ask the 'patient' to sit in a chair and the other to be the visitor to go and cheer them up. Ask them to change roles. Come into the circle to talk about the things they did and said.

Explain to children that when people have to leave home to go to hospital it is not like them leaving home to go on holiday or to go to college. They will be in a strange place with no family or friends around them. Their family will want to try to visit them if this can be arranged, but this will not always be possible. What could they do if they weren't able to visit them?

Ask the children to think about the rest of the family and how these people at home would feel if someone in their own family had to go to hospital. Ask volunteers to tell the class how they would feel if a person they loved had to go to stay in hospital.

Ask them to think about the space left behind when someone goes to hospital. Ask them to close their eyes and think of these spaces – a space at the table, a space in the bedroom, a space at bedtime, a space where they are not there to help everyone.

Tell them this story of Tim, whose Grandparents live with them at their house.

One day Grandma becomes ill and the doctor says she has to go to hospital. When Tim gets home from school, Grandma has already gone and Grandad is sitting by the fire feeling very sad and lonely. Tim misses his Grandma, because she does lots of things with him. When she is there, she plays cards, helps him with his homework, listens to him read and knits him jumpers. At teatime, there is a space at the table where she usually sits and when it's bedtime she is not there to read him a story. Tim is worried that Grandma could be so ill that she doesn't come home.

Ask the children to think of all the things they can do to help themselves to feel better about Grandma not being there. Ask them to 'question and answer': 'What will help Grandma? I could...'

Jot down these responses to make a list.

Tell the children the rest of the story.

Grandma is in hospital for two weeks and then she comes home again. Everyone is very happy and cheerful when she comes home. The chair isn't empty, the place at the table isn't empty, her bed isn't empty and she is part of the family again.

You could use the activity sheet, 'We Are Missing You' now.

I could...

make a card
get some flowers
take fruit
visit her
tell her things
make her laugh
cheer her up.

We Are Missing You

Draw Tim visiting his grandma in hospital.

What is he taking to the hospital?
He is taking

....

and

....

What is he saying?
He is saying

....

....

Turn over.
Draw the party when Grandma comes home. What will Tim say at the party? Write what he says to Grandma.

Come Home Soon

In Circle Time tell the children the story of Natasha, whose father has to work a long way away.

> Natasha lives with her father, mother and little brother in a small house in the country. She has always lived there and the family love their little house and the garden which is bursting with plants that Natasha's mother looks after. All the family is really happy there. But there is one thing that spoils it all. Natasha's dad is a geologist and has to work in other countries. Sometimes he goes away for a whole year, finding out things about the rocks and minerals there; sometimes he just goes for a week or so. When he goes for a whole year, he has two long holidays and Natasha loves this. Sometimes they can go out to the foreign country and visit him and Natasha loves this. Sometimes, in between jobs, he doesn't work at all and Natasha loves this. The only thing she doesn't love is when Dad has to go away.

Ask the children to think about how Natasha will feel about her dad being at home for long times and the times when he is away. Ask them to choose one of these sentences to finish: 'I think Natasha is unlucky because…' 'I think Natasha is lucky because…'

Jot down what the children say in two lists – the positive things that Natasha will like and the negative things that Natasha will not like.

Remind the children that Natasha's dad will also have good and bad feelings about missing Natasha. Can volunteers say what these are?

Natasha is lucky because…

her dad is home for long times
she can visit him abroad
her dad will bring her presents
he will write to her
she can send cards to her dad
she will know about other people.

Natasha is unlucky because…

he won't be there every day
he won't read her stories
he won't take her out
he won't play with her
he won't see her at school.

Talk with the children about the things that will help families where a parent has to work away from home for a long time. Explain that children grow up quickly and might forget what their parent looks and feels like. Tell them that a parent would not know how their child was growing and changing.

Ask them to think about how they can keep in touch with a parent who has to live abroad for a long time. Ask volunteers to give their good ideas for keeping in touch.

Talk to the children about those families where one parent is in one of the armed services. Ask if any have seen pictures on TV of ships coming home with lots of dads and mums on them waving to lots of families on the dockside? Can they give you words to describe how these people feel?

Ask the children how they would feel if a grown-up in their family had to go and work a long way from home. Explain the words 'advantage' and 'disadvantage' and ask them to think of both of these. Ask them to fold some paper in half and draw the advantages and disadvantages of having a parent who works abroad. You could read *Dear Daddy* by P. Dupasquier now before doing the activity sheet, 'Come Home Soon'.

Advantage	Disadvantage
We have exciting reunions.	We have sad partings.

Come Home Soon

Write a letter to your mum, dad, or a very special person. Write abut the things you'd miss doing together if they were not around.

Date
....

Dear

....

....

....

....

....

....

....

....

....

....

Turn over.

Draw a picture of you meeting this person after a long time apart.

Use a speech bubble to say how you are feeling.

What's the Matter, Kris?

In Circle Time tell the children about Kris.

Kris was a very quiet little boy in Year 1. He had two good friends and was quite good at his work. Then one day he came to school looking very miserable. His mum went into the classroom to talk to the teacher while Kris waited in the playground until it was time to go in. At his school they had a buddy system and his buddy, called James, was in Year 6. When James saw Kris crying in the playground he went over to him and said, 'Whatever's the matter Kris?' Kris looked up at his buddy and said that his mum and dad didn't love each other any more and were going to divorce and his dad was going to move away to live somewhere else. James sat down and talked to Kris and said he was sure that Kris' parents both loved him a lot and would let him spend a lot of time with each of them and they'd work things out so he wouldn't feel so bad. James said he would be there to talk to him at playtime.

Explain to the children that sometimes mums and dads decide to separate and live in different places, but that doesn't mean that they stop loving their children. When parents separate it's always because of their own feelings towards each other, not towards their children. They will have thought about it for a long time before they do anything.

How do the children think that Kris will be feeling on this Monday morning? Ask the children to finish the sentence: 'I think Kris will be feeling…'

Ask the children to think of what the children in Kris' class can say and do to help Kris to feel a bit better. Ask volunteers to raise a hand and tell you so that you can make a list. Talk about these ideas. Will they all work?

Kris is feeling…

sad
upset
angry
worried
anxious
lonely
nervous
fearful
it's his fault.

Ask the children to think of what Kris himself can do to feel better about this family upset. Ask them to draw a picture of Kris doing something that will make him feel a bit better and to write what he is doing.

Ask the children to bring their pictures to the circle and to 'stand and show'.

Talk about the kinds of things the children suggest and ask them if these things would work – would they make Kris feel a bit better?

Now ask the children to work in pairs to write a list of all the things they themselves do to help them to feel better when they are sad or angry about things. Come together in the circle and put their lists together to make one list. Display this list under the heading 'Ways

Kris is talking to his buddy

to Feel Cheerful' and ask the children to draw smiley faces to display around it.

Remind the children that it is not Kris' fault that his parents have decided to part. Remind them, too, that it won't matter what he does, he won't be able to make them come together again unless they want to. Ask the children to think of some good things that could happen to Kris in the years to come, if his parents stay apart. Things such as:

- having two lots of birthdays, one with Dad and one with Mum
- going to different places on holiday
- having two bedrooms and two sets of toys
- outings with Dad and outings with Mum.

You could read *Are We Nearly There?* by L. Baum and talk about this story with the children before asking them to do the activity sheet, 'What's the Matter Kris?'.

What's the Matter, Kris?

Draw Kris going on an outing with his dad. Write in the speech bubble to say how Kris is feeling.

This is Kris with his dad at

....

Turn over.
Draw Kris on an outing with his mum and write what they are doing.

Different Kinds of Families

Explain to the children that there are many kinds of families; families with no father, families with no mother, families with no mother or father. Explain to the children that in some families where parents have divorced one of the children lives with one parent and other children live with the other. Tell them this story of Bethany.

> Bethany lives with her mother in a flat in London where Mummy has a job in a hospital. A year ago, when Bethany was five years old, Dad went away to live and work in Birmingham and took her brother Jack to live with him.
>
> Sometimes Jack comes to visit them in London and sometimes Bethany goes to visit Jack and her father. Bethany loves her mother and her father and especially she loves her brother Jack.
>
> She still misses them both a lot and wishes that they could all live together again, but whenever she talks about this to either of her parents they just say that this is not possible. This makes Bethany very sad; she wants her brother and Dad to be there all the time. Whenever Bethany has a wish – like when she got the wishbone from the Christmas turkey, or when she blew out the candles on her cake, she always makes the same wish, 'I wish we could all live together again.' She sometimes wonders if it is her fault that they don't. When she went to visit Jack, they once talked about this and Jack said that he wondered if it were his fault. Their parents try to keep them both happy in their new homes, but Bethany is still very sad and keeps wishing…

Ask the children to think about Bethany's wish. What do they think it is? Ask them to put up a hand if they think it will ever come true. Ask volunteers to say why they think this.

Ask volunteers who think it will not come true to tell you why they think this.

> I think Bethany keeps wishing that her Mum and Dad will live together again.

Ask children to raise a hand if they think it is Bethany's fault that her parents don't live together. Ask those who raise a hand to say why they think this.

Explain that it is never the children's fault if parents decide to live in different places and tell the children that there is nothing that Bethany can do to make her parents choose to live together.

Ask the children to think about what Bethany can do to help herself to feel less unhappy about her family situation. Ask them to work in pairs and talk about the things that Bethany can do. Ask them to work together to make a picture with Bethany in the middle and to draw around her the things she can do to make her feel happier and not so sad.

Explain that Bethany is lucky that she still has two parents and a brother. She sees them often and they are still family. Remind the children that there are lots of different kinds of families and that this is only one kind. Can they tell you of some of the different kinds of families they have seen on TV or in storybooks?

You could use the activity sheet, 'Different Kinds of Families' now.

Different Kinds of Families

Draw all your family – the people who live in your house.
Write the names of all the people.

This is my family. Their names are.

....

....

....

Turn over.
Imagine and draw a different kind of family and write their names.
Write about this imaginary family.

Claire's Family

In Circle Time tell the children this story about Claire whose parents separated when she was a baby.

> When Claire was only two years old her parents had a big disagreement and decided to separate. Claire's mum got a job and she couldn't look after a baby so Claire's dad took her to live with his own parents who lived quite a way away. Claire's grandma was happy to have a baby girl, because all her children had been boys. Grandpa decorated a bedroom in a pinky colour with a border of toys all around it and they put some of Claire's old toys and some new ones there for her. While Claire was very small, her dad came to visit her most weekends, and sometimes her mum came to take her out instead. Claire was really happy; she had three homes and three families. When Claire was three she started at the playschool in the nearby school and when she was four she went into the school itself. When Claire was five, her dad came to live and work very near to her grandparents and she started to sleep at her dad's house. She loved both her mum and her dad to bits and did wish they would live together again as one family. She was always very sad when her mum brought her back from a visit and she had to say goodbye. She would just cry and cry. The next day at school she would be sad all day.

Ask the children what they would say to Claire when was sad and cried when she left one parent. Ask them to finish the sentence: 'I would say…'

Ask them to think what Claire could do to stop feeling sad and make herself feel better. Ask volunteers to say what they think. Jot down what they say to make a list. Read out the list and discuss their suggestions. Would they work?

Tell the children the rest of Claire's story.

Claire could...

stop crying
cuddle her Dad
talk about it
watch TV
read a book
play a game
have a drink and biscuit
remember the visit
think of her friends
look forward to next time.

When Claire was six her dad went to school one open day and talked to Claire's teacher about her work. Later he met Claire's teacher outside school and they became friends. When Claire was seven, her dad and the teacher were married and Claire went to live with them in their new house. Claire's mum still came to take her out sometimes or took her home to her house at the weekend. When Claire was eight, her dad told her that she was going to have a baby sister. The year after that she had a baby brother and the next year another sister. She loved these three children and missed them when she visited her mum. When Claire was twelve her mum said that she was going to get married to a man who had three children – twin six year old boys and a four year old little girl. Claire still lived at her dad's and visited her mum every month. Suddenly she belonged to two big families, with six step-brothers and sisters.

Ask the children to think about Claire's new family.

How do they think she felt when her dad told her about a new baby sister? Ask the children to 'pass the face'. How did she feel when her mum decided to get married again? Ask them to finish the sentence, 'I think Claire would feel…'

Would she worry that her mum wouldn't love her any more? What would they say to her about this? Explain that the love that her mum had for Claire would not be less just because she had step-children to love.

How do they think Claire felt when she had new step-brothers and sisters? Ask the children to work in pairs to talk about the good things and the not so good things about having step-brothers and sisters. Ask them to make two lists to share with everyone in Circle Time.

You could read *Grace & Family* by M. Hoffman and C. Binch and *The Visitors who Came to Stay* by A. McAfee to the children before asking them to do the activity sheet, 'Claire's Family'.

The good things are…

lots of brothers and sisters
two families to love
being the big one in both families
being able to help with the little ones
two Christmas family parties
lots of grandparents.

Claire's Family

Draw Claire and her dad in the middle of this triangle.
Draw her two little sisters and brother in the ovals.

How do you think Claire feels in this family?
I think Claire feels

....

....

Turn over.
Draw Claire with her mum and her other step-family.
Write what she can do to help her mum with the twins and
the little girl.

Life Has to Go On

Start with the picture book *Always and Forever* by Alan Durant.

Read the story straight through with the children. It is about four animals who live in a little house in the woods. All the animals work together and they have a happy life there. Otter is the cook, Mole mends things, Hare looks after the garden and Fox is like their father; he loves them all very much. One day Fox dies and the animals are all very sad and upset. They keep missing Fox and are all so miserable they can't think of anything else. They stay indoors crying and feeling sad. Then Squirrel comes to visit. She wants to know where they have been all winter and tries to cheer them up. She says that life has to go on. As the animals begin to talk about Fox they remember all the happy and funny little things Fox had done. They make a special garden with a bench where they can sit and remember Fox. They feel as though Fox is still with them as father of their house.

Talk with the children about animals being born and living and getting old and dying. Remind them that it was OK for the animals to feel sad when Fox died. They cried because they wanted him to still be there with them and they missed him so very much.

Ask the children to close their eyes and think about the story and about what the animals did when Fox died. Ask them to finish the sentence: 'When Fox died…' Jot down what the children say, allowing them to pass and asking those who repeat to change places with the person who said it last.

When Fox died

They all cried.
They buried Fox.
They missed him.
Their hearts ached.
It was winter.
They talked about Fox.
Then they were silent.

Ask volunteers to raise a hand if they can remember what Squirrel said in the springtime when she came to visit them. Ask volunteers to tell you what Otter did to welcome Squirrel. Ask them to raise a hand to tell you some of the funny things about Fox that the animals remembered. Ask them to raise a hand if they can tell you what the animals made in memory of Fox, so that they could remember him.

Ask them to form groups of five and practise role-playing the story before asking one group to show their role-play to the class.

Explain to the children that when someone goes away, leaves us or dies, it is OK to be sad but we must remember we can't change these things. As Squirrel said, 'Life has to go on.'

Explain that, just as the animals did, we, too, can do things to remember people who are no longer with us.

Can the children think of things we can do so that we don't forget people who have gone away or died?

To remember people we can...

think about them
think about things we did
look at photos
talk about them
remember their jokes
draw things that they did
remember what they did
keep their picture in your head
keep things they gave us
plant a 'remembering' tree.

Ask them to work in pairs and write down all the things they can think of that people can do to remember people who have gone away or died. Ask them to share their list with their group and make one list. Ask volunteers to read their list to the class.

Read and enjoy *Always and Forever* once again, without stopping for comments or explanations before asking the children to complete the activity sheet, 'Life Has to Go On'.

Life Has to Go On

Draw Mole, Otter and Hare feeling sad about missing Fox. Draw Squirrel coming to visit them.

What are they doing to remember Fox?
They are

....

....

....

Turn over.
Draw the garden they have made and the bench. Write one funny thing they remember about Fox.

A Memory Box

Tell the children the story of Sam, who was so very ill and knew that he was going to die.

Jason's big brother Sam was very ill. The doctors had tried so very hard to make him better, but there was no cure for his illness. Every day he got sicker and sicker in hospital and had to stay in bed all day. One day the doctor said that Sam could go home to stay with his family for the rest of his life. They brought Sam home in an ambulance and Jason was overjoyed to see him. He stayed at Sam's bedside all day and talked to him, listened to him and helped him with his meals.

Jason somehow knew that Sam was going to die soon, and talked to his mother about it. They began to talk about all the things the family had done together before Sam had become ill. Sam tried to join in the talk, but mostly he just listened and sometimes he smiled.

Jason's mother brought out old photographs about schooldays and holidays and Jason said that they should find all the good ones with Sam in them and keep them in a special memory box. Sam helped them to decide which to keep. Then Jason said they could put other things in the box – things to help them remember Sam's football days; his school report when he was ten. They found some badges to put in and some birthday cards. They found pictures that Sam had drawn. They found Sam's bobble hat that he wore when he went to football matches. All these things went into the memory box because they wanted to keep these things safe to help to keep Sam alive in their hearts.

Sam's memory box

photos of Sam
medals or certificates
a game or picture he likes
pictures he drew
a school book
praise from a teacher/ friend
a postcard he sent
favourite music CD
a poster from his bedroom
a letter he wrote to his family.

Ask the children to think of any other things that could go into Sam's memory box. Make a list of these.

Ask the children if they ever ask their parents or other people in their family about what it was like when they were young children. Ask some volunteers, tell the class. Tell them that one day they will want to remember their own childhood so that they can tell other people what it was like. Ask them to think about what they would put in a memory box to remember their childhood when they are grown up.

Ask them to think of one thing and to finish the sentence: 'I would put… into my memory box.' Collect their responses to make a list. Discourage children from 'passing'. Read out their list.

Ask the children to close their eyes and think of one person in their family. What would be good to keep so that they can easily remember this person when they themselves are grown up? Ask them to think of other people in their family and good things to remember them by. Ask them to get paper and crayons and to draw one thing to remember each person in their family by. Ask them to write the name of the person underneath each drawing. Ask them to write a sentence about the one person they most want to remember when they are grown up.

Remind them of the story of Sam and the memory box that Jason made so that they could remember him. Remind then that it's OK to cry when someone dies.

Read *Wilfred Gordon McDonald Partridge* by M. Fox about how he helps Miss Nancy to find her lost memories, before asking them to do the activity sheet, 'A Memory Box'.

I would put my…

teddy
Gameboy
best game
Harry Potter book
sweet wrapper
Lego
new shoes
notebook
a feather from the budgie
a bit of hair from the hamster

A Memory Box

Fill this memory box with all the things you want to remember when you are grown up.

Wordbox

holiday

visit

london

circus

theatre

aeroplane

train

Turn over.

Draw and write about your most precious memory.

Write about the one special thing that you want to remember always and forever.

A New Life

In Circle Time tell the children the story of Amjid who left his own country to come to England.

Amjid is seven when he starts school in England. He can't speak much English and his new school seems strange to him and so do the boys and girls there. Amjid works very hard to learn English and after one term he can speak quite well. One day in Circle Time he tells his story to the class… He left his country in a great hurry because people were coming to catch his family and put them in prison or even kill them. His mother, father and he quickly packed a few things and some food and walked to the edge of their village. There, a battered lorry picked them up and drove off into the country. For six days they didn't stop for anything, just hid in the lorry and ate and slept. Then they arrived at the sea. Amjid had never seen the sea before and it frightened him. They waited a whole week for a boat to bring them to England. Then they had to wait in line for ages for Father to show their papers that said they could come to live in Britain. Amjid cried when he told his story and said he missed his old home and his friends there. He missed such a lot, but his parents said that they were very lucky to be safe.

Talk to the children about people who have to run away from their homes because they are afraid. Explain that Britain is seen as a good, safe place to live and that many people would like to live here. Tell children that only some people are allowed to come and stay, some come and stay for a little while and go to school here, others try to come, but are sent home because there isn't room for everyone.

Ask the children to think about how Amjid felt when he had to leave his home and everyone he knew in the middle of the night and run away to another country. Ask them to finish the sentence: 'Amjid would feel…'

Amjid would feel…

worried
sad
afraid
scared
unhappy
anxious
frightened
nervous
excited.

Remind the children how lucky we are in Britain to have safe homes and families or guardians to look after us. Remind them that in this country the government tries to make sure that people have somewhere to live, are safe, have enough to eat, have schools to go to and can have help from doctors and hospitals when they are sick. Explain that people in other countries are not so lucky.

Ask the children to think about what they could do if Amjid had come to your school and told his story to them. What could they do to help him to know that it is OK to feel sad? Ask them to finish the sentence: 'I could...' Jot down what the children say and read through their list. Ask them to try to decide the very best thing to do. Ask them to 'vote with their feet' and jot down how many agree on the best things to do.

Ask the children to think about the best thing to say to Amjid to help him to feel welcome and wanted in this country. Ask children to work together in their groups to compose and write down one sentence. Ask a volunteer from each group to tell you their sentence and jot down the important elements of each one. Read through all the sentences and ask the children to help you to make one combined sentence that encapsulates the best elements from the list.

Talk about organising a 'Circle of Friends' to support Amjid at school if he begins to feel sad and insecure. What could these friends do and say to help him to settle down and feel happy in this country?

Could the children organise a 'Circle of Friends'? How would they do it? Who could help?

You could use the activity sheet, 'A New Life' now.

The best thing to do is...

be friendly
show Amjid around
be a good buddy to him
show how things are here
play with him
talk to him
make sure he joins in.

The best thing to say is...

It's OK to feel sad and miss things but we will help you to like it here.

A New Life

Draw the things that you would miss most if you had to leave everything and move to a new country.

The things I would miss most are

....

....

....

....

Turn over.
Draw yourself leaving your home and all these things behind.
Write how you would feel in your new country.

When Grandpa Died

Start with the picture book *Read Grandpa's Slide Show* by G. Gould.

Read the story straight through with the children. It's about Douglas' visits to his grandparents and how the visits always ended with Grandpa giving a slide show. Then Grandpa died and now Grandma lives alone. When they first visited Grandma everyone was very sad but before they left they had a slide show and although this was different now, it helped them to remember the good times in Grandpa's life.

Ask the children to think of the main parts of this story. Ask volunteers to remind you of the stages in the story. Make a list of these and number them in order. Ask the children to work in their groups, choose one of the numbers and make a picture about that part of the story about Grandpa's slide show.

1. Grandpa showed his slides
2. They all watched
3. Then Grandpa died
4. Everyone was very sad.
5. They had a funeral
6. They went to Grandma's
7. They had another slide show.

Put all the pictures in order with the numbered sentences that tell the story. Display this in the classroom as one long strip picture. Talk about the feelings of each of the people in the pictures and ask the children to suggest 'feelings' speech bubbles to add to the picture, for example, Grandpa could say, 'I feel happy showing you my slides,' in picture 1.

Talk to the children about each of the pictures, being sensitive to anyone who might have been bereaved. Ask them how they would have felt if they had been there or if it had been their Grandad. Ask them to finish one of these sentences, either: 'If I had been there I would have felt…' or 'If it had been my Grandad I would have felt…' Change places for repeats.

Ask the children to think of an old person in their family.

Ask them to close their eyes and think about what they would miss most about this person if they went away or died, like Douglas' grandpa. Ask them to finish the sentence: 'If...wasn't there, I would miss...'

I would miss...

talking to them
them reading to me
them taking us out
at my birthday tea
Christmas with them
babysitting me
looking after me
going to their house
playing cards with them
making cakes with them
doing my knitting
helping me to sew
watching me at football.

Discourage children from passing and at the end talk about the various responses from the children.

Ask the children to think of what they do for this old person to show that they love them. Ask volunteers to say what they do, for example, do they visit them, play with them, give a present on birthdays? Jot down and make a list of what the volunteers say.

In Circle Time ask the children to 'pass a face' to show how they would feel if this person went away or died.

Ask the children to think of something that makes them happy when they are with this old person. Ask volunteers to tell you about one time when they were with this old person and something funny happened and they and the old person had a good laugh together.

Ask the children to think of one thing they would remember most about this old person. Ask them to finish the sentence: 'I would remember...'

Remind the children that all people will die someday, that it is OK to feel sad but that we have to remember the good things about being with them.

Ask the children to do the activity sheet, 'When Grandpa Died' now.

When Grandpa Died

Draw your Grandma or Grandpa or some other old person in your family.
Write their name on the line.

....

The things I like about

....

are

....

....

....

Turn over.
Draw yourself with this person the last time you saw them.
Write about what you did.

A Terrible Accident

In Circle Time tell the children this story about Harry's accident.

Harry was 20 years old and liked to run. He went out running every evening after work. One evening he was running along the side of the road when a car came around the corner and knocked him down. The man in the car stopped and came to see how Harry was. When he saw that he was badly hurt, he dialled 999 on his mobile and called the ambulance. Harry was taken to hospital where the doctors tried very hard to make him better. He was in a coma, just like being asleep but he couldn't wake up. Harry's family went to see him every day but he didn't wake up. They tried all kinds of things to try to wake him; reading to him, playing his favourite music, talking about good times. One day the doctor spoke to his parents about Harry's injuries and said they didn't think that Harry would ever wake up. He said that the family must try to get used to the idea of life without Harry. Three days later Harry died. His little brother Will cried when they told him and said that it would never be the same without Harry.

Talk to the children about road accidents and how careful we all have to be when walking or running on or near roads. Explain what a coma is and how sometimes people wake up and are quite well but that sometimes others who are badly hurt inside die after quite a long time.

Ask children to work in large groups to role-play the accident, the ambulance and arrival at the hospital.

Ask the children to think about how Will felt when Harry died. Ask them to 'pass the face'. Ask them to finish this sentence: 'Will would be feeling...' Jot down their words and when everyone has had their turn read out the list.

Will felt...

like crying
sad
unhappy
alone
worried
lonely
lost
friendless.

Ask the children to think about the changes in the house with one brother not there any more. What would they all miss about Harry? Ask them to think about Will and what he would miss when Harry was not there any more. Ask volunteers to tell the class.

Ask the children to think about the things Will could do so that he would not feel so sad about Harry. Ask them to work in pairs and to draw pictures of some of the things Will could do. Ask them to show their pictures to their group and to choose the best ideas to put on one sheet of paper. They can cut out the pictures too and glue them on. Ask them to write some speech bubbles of what Will could say and to put these around their pictures.

Will would miss...

Harry at mealtimes
playing with him
telling him things
talking about running
reading to him
Harry's music
Harry's jokes
telling about school
playing jokes on Mum
cleaning the car with him.

Come together in a circle and ask one spokesperson from each group to tell the class about the collage they have made. Talk about the ideas the children have illustrated and which will work best. Have they thought about Will collecting memories of Harry to put in a memory box or a memory book? Have they thought about Will writing down some of the good times they had together? Have they thought about Will collecting some of Harry's music CDs to listen to or making a display of Will's running medals and certificates to look at?

Remind the children that it is OK to be sad when someone dies, that everyone will always miss someone they love and that there are really good ways to keep the memory of the person alive. Remind them that as long as Will's family talk about the things that Harry did and loved and played they will keep the memory of him alive.

Ask the children to complete the activity sheet, 'A Terrible Accident' now.

A Terrible Accident

Draw Will thinking about watching Harry win a race.

Will is thinking about

....

....

....

Turn over.
Draw Will making a memory box. Write about two things he will put in it.

Picture storybooks

All these stories have a great deal to offer children as good stories in themselves and you can use them as a way in for discussion about loss, grief and bereavement. Those marked with * have been used as the story for an activity.

Alborough, J. (1994) *Where's My Teddy?* Walker
Eddy has lost his Teddy, Freddy, so off he goes into the dark and horrible wood to find him. At the same time a gigantic bear has lost his Teddy...

Baum, L. (1986) *Are We Nearly There?* Bodley Head
Simon and his dad are on their way home after a day out together. Dad leaves Simon with Mum and Simon waves Dad goodbye.

Burningham, J. (1988) *Granpa.* Picture Puffin
When Granpa dies a little girl is left with wonderful memories of a very special friendship.

Dupasquier, P. (2002) *Dear Daddy.* Anderson Press
Sophie writes to her father who is away at sea. What she says in her letters is illustrated and above these pictures are others showing what Daddy is doing. Eventually Daddy comes home and on the last page they are reunited.

* Durant, A. (2003) *Always and Forever.* Doubleday
When Fox dies, his friends think they will never get over their sadness, but when Squirrel calls, she reminds them of all the funny things Fox did and they realise that Fox is still in their hearts and memories and will be with them forever.

Fox, M. (1984) *Wilfred Gordon McDonald Partridge.* Picture Puffins
Miss Nancy has lost her memory and Wilfred Gordon McDonald Partridge tries to help her find it. A book about memories.

* Gould, G. (1987) *Grandpa's Slide Show.* Puffin
Grandpa always showed a slide show whenever Douglas visited. Then Grandpa died and things were different and Douglas and his family felt very sad. The next time they visited Grandma they had the slide show again and shared memories of Grandpa.

Hathorn, L. (1995) *Grandma's Shoes.* Viking

A book about a family healing from the death of a loved one. Recovering from such grief can take a long time.

Hoffman, M. & Binch, C. (1995) *Grace and Family.* Frances Lincoln

Grace lives with Ma, Nana and a cat called Paw-Paw. Then Papa asks her to visit him in the Gambia and she meets a whole new family.

* Hughes, S. (1977) *Dogger.* Picture Lions

When Dave loses his best toy, the only one he takes to bed with him, he searches everywhere, only to find it the next day on a stall at the school fair. Before he can buy it, someone else does, and how he gets it back shows how much his sister loves him.

Limb, S. & Munoz, C. (1995) *Come Back Grandma.* Red Fox

Bessie is very upset at the death of her beloved Grandma. It takes a long time; until she is grown up and has a daughter just like Grandma.

McAfee, A. (1984) *Visitors Who Came to Stay,* Hamish Hamilton

How it feels when a parent meets someone new to love and wants to make one whole new family from two separate ones.

* Robinson, C. & Broadley, S. (1994) *Leaving Mrs Ellis.* Bodley Head

A story about Leo who will be moving on to a new class and the loss he feels in leaving behind a loving teacher.

√ **Selway, M. (1993) *Don't Forget to Write.* Red Fox**

Rosie is going to stay with Grandad and Aunty Mabel and doesn't want to go. She writes letters to her family which start off with her wanting to come home immediately and end up with her wanting to stay a little longer.

Simonds, P. (1989) *Fred.* Penguin

Lazy old Fred was just an ordinary cat, until he died and had the funeral of the century. A light hearted story of the death and funeral of Fred, the superstar cat.

Varley, S. (1992) *Badger's Parting Gifts.* Julia McRae

When Badger dies, all his animal friends find it hard not to be sad, until they all realise they have a special memory of Badger. He had given each of them a parting gift that will help them to remember him for ever.

Waddell, M. (1990) *Grandma's Bill.* Simon & Schuster

Bill didn't know he had a Grandpa until he saw a photo when he visited Grandma. Grandma explained that he too had been called Bill and brought out the photo album and shared all her memories with young Bill. Bill and Grandma look together at the pictures of the past and the present, sharing the reassuring sense of continuity.

Waddell, M. (1991) *Once There Were Giants.* Walker

A lovely story about the circle of life – baby growing up, moving on, leaving home and a new baby.

Weninger, B. & Marks, A. (1995) *Goodbye Daddy!* North-South

A story about separation and divorce. Tommy is upset because Daddy lives in another house now and has to go to his home after a day out. Teddy tells him a story which helps…

* Wilhelm, H. (1985) *I'll Always Love You.* Hodder & Stoughton

A story of the close relationship between a boy and his dog and how he comes to terms with its death. Effie the dog grew quickly, grew old, became ill and died. The boy's grief is tempered with the knowledge that he had repeatedly told his dog, 'I'll always love you.'

Resources

Bornman, J., Collins, M. & Maines, B. (2004) *Just the Same on the Inside.* London: Paul Chapman Books.

Collins, M. (2001) *Circle Time for the Very Young.* Bristol: Lucky Duck Publishing Ltd.

Collins, M. (2001) *Because We're Worth It*. Bristol: Lucky Duck Publishing Ltd.

Collins, M. (2002) *Circling Round Citizenship*. Bristol: Lucky Duck Publishing Ltd.

Collins, M. (2002) *Because I'm Special.* Bristol: Lucky Duck Publishing Ltd.

Collins, M. (2003) *Enhancing Circle Time for the Very Young*. Bristol: Lucky Duck Publishing Ltd.

Collins, M. (2004) *Circling Safely*. Bristol: Lucky Duck Publishing Ltd.

DfEE (2001) *Promoting Children's Mental Health within Early Years and School Settings*.

Collins, M. (2004) *But is it Bullying?* London: Paul Chapman Publishing.

DATE DUE
